NEW ASIAN INTERIORS

KENGO KUMA

Designed by Kengo Kuma

This traditional Japanese house has been renovated and extended, with the addition of a pavilion suite, by the great Japanese architect Kengo Kuma. Emphasizing the relationship between building and landscape, Kuma has concealed the structure, setting it harmoniously within an ancient garden full of symbolic references, and enriched it further with the addition of movable walls to achieve greater fluidity between the rooms. The garden thus becomes an extension of the house, an interweaving of nature and the domestic space.

Above A grid of stones on the surface of the water leads to the tea house and the new pavilion.

Right The stone floor and glass walls of the pavilion give a sense of continuity between interior and exterior.

Above A narrow strip of water separates the new pavilion and the tea house. The garden can be glimpsed beyond.

Overleaf The space in the restructured main building is clearly delineated by the strict grid of modular tatami mats, measuring 180 x 90 centimetres each.

Opposite, top The new pavilion, as seen from the tea house.

Opposite, bottom Although wood, stone and glass have been used in a modern way, as seen here in the new pavilion, they are materials connected with tradition.

Left, above A narrow path divides the tea house from the pond.

Left, below A stone lantern stands imposingly at the edge of the small pond in the garden.

Opposite The newly built bathroom, with its hard, stone edges softened by a cascade of greenery.

MASSIMO LISTRI

NEW
ASIAN
INTERIORS

Text by Nicoletta del Buono
With 327 color illustrations

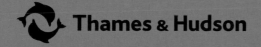

Thames & Hudson

NEW ASIAN INTERIORS

Contemporary Western culture does not like to analyze; it rarely dwells upon details, however illuminating they might be, and tends to ignore differences, half-tones and shadows. It prefers to use generalizations and too often slots things into categories, leaning towards simplification, unjustified assimilation and banal labels.

This tendency to simplify is particularly noticeable when it comes to the houses and interiors of Asian countries. Minimalism is 'Zen', for example, the atmosphere is 'oriental', spaces are 'as refined as a haiku', the decoration has a 'touch of the Mandarin' about it, and the furniture is from such-and-such dynasty, despite the fact that each dynasty lasted for centuries and contained a succession of generations of masters and manufacturers. The adjectives 'Chinese', 'Japanese' and 'Indian' are used as if discussing the inhabitants of a medieval Tuscan town, who are all the same as each other yet completely different from their neighbours (the fourteenth-century denizens of Siena and Florence, say). But behind those adjectives lies much greater complexity; thousand-year-old cultures with amazingly different facets linked not only to the passing of time, but also to the countless places and civilizations that influenced them.

Fortunately, the photographs inside this book re-establish the expressive and intellectual strength of the differences between the many Chinas, Indias and Japans.

Visiting the houses and recording them with his inquisitive lens, photographer Massimo Listri is always interested in more than outer surfaces, and shows how living in Tokyo is different from living in Kyoto, the many ways of interpreting the domestic landscape in Beijing, the abyss between Jakarta and Bali, and the flowering of the varying lifestyles in Thailand. Although there has been a strong movement advocating the return to traditional housing, there is still an intense attraction towards modernity, even Western modernity, albeit assimilated into the local culture.

As Listri is both an artist and a consummate cultural recorder, he does not juxtapose photographs en masse, but moves house by house, interior by interior, to build up an anthropological picture that takes into account the distinctive features of each artifact and its context, inviting us to see the aesthetic, cultural and historical details, and perhaps even understand them. Each page is alive with both exotic charm and scientific precision; it records, describes and classifies, leaving us with the pleasure, rather than the chore, of having ideas and reaching conclusions about the multi-faceted world of Asia and its many lifestyles and architectural traditions, both old and new.

MASSIMO LISTRI

Designed by Marianna Gagliardi

Left A Vietnamese red lacquer tray and purple paper fan form a colourful contrast to the black and green silk covering of the day bed.

Right The floor of the terrace, overlooking the Chao Phraya River, is made of teak, edged by a parapet of dark grey steel. The Diamond chairs are by Harry Bertoia for Knoll.

Overleaf On the floor in front of the nineteenth-century Chinese day bed is an Anatolian rug of the same vintage.

The Bangkok apartment of Massimo Listri, the well-known artist and photographer, and the creative force behind the pictures in this book, overlooks the majestic Chao Phraya River, in one of the few residential buildings in the area that is not a hotel. The space, comprising one hundred square metres and lit by a seven-metre-high wall of glass, has been restructured by interior designer Marianna Gagliardi. She removed the old floor, opting for a new one in dark teak, and chose a palette of green, white and black against which to display the owner's collection of Khmer sculptures and oriental arts and crafts.

Above A nineteenth-century Chinese sculpture, representing a warrior deity, perches atop a console table.

Left The artwork at the far end of the living room is a twelfth-century Khmer relief. On the pedestal to the right is a sculpture from the same period.

Above A large teak bookcase in the living room displays fifteenth-century Tibetan teapots, pieces of Vietnamese lacquer, and small Chinese terracotta sculptures from the Tang dynasty (618–907).

Opposite, above A stone-and-lacquer Buddha's head from Burma, dating from the eighteenth century.

Opposite, below The Laotian gong is a striking decorative element.

Above Celadon-green glass basins set into a teak surround inject a dash of colour against bathroom walls that have been covered with slabs of lava rock, cut to resemble tiles.

Right The four-poster bed in the master bedroom is covered with Uzbek blankets, while two nineteenth-century Chinese armchairs rest against the wall.

A HOUSE AT BUKIT

On the Indonesian island of Sumatra, a typical Minangkabau house known as a *rumah gadang* has been painstakingly repaired and restored to its ancient splendour by Carlo Pessina. The Milanese artist and designer was also responsible for the traditional furnishings, which were sourced from all over Indonesia. The distinctive features of *rumah gadang* houses include extremely steep gabled roofs, occasionally shaped like bisons' horns at the ends; sumptuous, highly coloured external carvings; verandas that run along the front of the house and are used for social activities and for meals; and raised foundations.

Above A front view of the *rumah gadang*, decorated with carved botanical motifs, all of which have symbolic meaning.

Opposite The open second floor of the house – almost a covered roof terrace – looks directly out over the Indian Ocean.

Above The pigments and decorative carvings of the foundation pillars are all original.

Left The 'horned' shape of the roof is a relic of the Minangkabau culture of Sumatra. Although Islamic in appearance, the animistic reference is Hindu in origin. Luxuriant tropical vegetation flourishes in the garden.

The carved teak staircase going up to
the first floor of the *rumah gadang* is
also typical of the Sumatran tradition.

The open colonnade of the ground
floor is now used as a place to eat and
socialize in the sunshine.

Above Through the entrance is a view of the garden, filled with palms and exotic plants.

Right Inside, the house seems much more austere than the elaborately carved exterior would suggest. In the first-floor bedroom, the wood plank walls have been painted white, and Sumba *ikat* blankets cover the bed.

The roof of the second-floor master bedroom is thatched with *kunai* grass. Chairs, furnishings and other objects were specially sourced from across Indonesia, and chosen to complement the style of the *rumah gadang*.

JANYA AND PORNTHEP ATTAKANWONG

Designed by Pornthep Attakanwong

Left A wooden sculpture of Bodhisattva Guanyin from the Ming dynasty (1368–1644). Behind it, a nineteenth-century Chinese tapestry can be seen.

Right A view of the formally appointed living room.

Overleaf In the same room, on the right, is a sixth-century statue of Buddha from Thailand.

Janya and Pornthep Attakanwong's home in Bangkok, designed by Pornthep, was devised to show off the owners' splendid collection of oriental statues. The house is like a museum in miniature, with its series of galleries, teak panels and masonry walls broken up by display niches, and the works of sculpture take guests on a wonderful journey from the Mekong to the valley of the Burmese temples of Pagan, bringing these ancient splendours to life in a domestic arena.

Above A gilded statue of a Buddha, from China, stands in a niche, facing away from the corridor.

Opposite The eleventh-century Cambodian stone torso is a harmonious counterpoint to the nineteenth-century Tibetan silk rugs.

Right Two enthroned deities from the Qing dynasty (1644–1911) keep watch in the living room, next to a nineteenth-century wood and alabaster chair.

Opposite In the master bedroom, nineteenth-century Tibetan rugs sit atop floorboards of tropical wood. On the wall above the bed head is a painting from Vietnam.

GERALD PIERCE

Having been sent to Bangkok on what was meant to be a short business trip, Gerald Pierce, art director of the Jim Thompson advertising agency, fell in love with the place and soon made it his home. Pierce's house is full of contradictions, where high-tech and traditional, Western design and Eastern art, and antiques from Europe, China and Burma all sit happily together.

Right On a shelf painted indigo blue sits a small bronze Buddha from the Ayutthaya period (1351–1767).

Opposite A Gustavian day bed and two French period chairs sound a European note next to a pair of wood Akha 'guardians' from Luangnamtha, in Laos.

Left The kitchen is dominated by two wooden 'guardians' from northern Thailand. Set against the ultra-modern appliances, on the wall near the cooker hood is a bronze nineteenth-century gong from Attapeu, in Laos.

Above The walls and false ceiling are covered in wooden joists, which form a 'sandwich' where wiring is concealed.

Above The master bedroom is furnished with simple Swedish designs.

Right In the master bathroom, a gilded bronze bust of a Burmese Buddha from the Mandalay period faces the hydromassage bath.

Left Gustavian furniture and pale wood panelling contrast with the dark shades and geometric motifs of Naga textiles.

Opposite Art enriches even the smallest spaces in the house. In a corner of the hallway, the figure of a wooden Akha 'guardian' from Chiang Rai in northern Thailand perches atop a pedestal.

Overleaf The torso of a fifteenth-century Ayutthaya Buddha from Thailand stands on a simply shaped console table made from black lacquered wood. Behind it, the sliding doors of the cabinet open to reveal antiques from across the Indochinese peninsula and China.

MAISON BERABAN

Designed by Renato Guillermo de Pola

Located in the residential area of Seminyak, this two-storey villa, topped with a glass pyramid, was entirely designed by Renato Guillermo de Pola, who was also responsible for the interior design, the enchanting lighting, and the winter garden of tropical plants. Furniture and soft furnishings were all made using local materials by Javanese and Balinese craftsmen.

Above The glass staircase – a rarity in Bali – leads up from the winter garden to the mezzanine, under the cupola.

Opposite An enormous chandelier hangs from the pyramid-shaped glass roof. The villa occupies 250 square metres.

Below and right The floor in the large, first-floor living room is made of teak planks, separated by strips of illuminated pebbles. The sofas and other furniture were made to de Pola's design.

Above In a corner of the living room, an artwork by de Pola that incorporates a recycled Vespa scooter hangs above the sofa. On the left, the glass staircase leads up through the winter garden.

Opposite The lush winter garden, full of tropical plants.

Overleaf Everything in the house was made by local craftsmen to the architect's design.

The dining room and stainless-steel kitchen. On the left is an artwork by de Pola, made from enormous painted bamboo canes and enclosed in a glass box. The table and dining chairs were also designed by the architect, and are made of teak.

The beautiful bed linen and fabrics that adorn the master bedroom have all been locally made. The bathroom can be glimpsed in the background.

HELEN VON BÜREN

Garden by Michael White

Amidst the green vegetation of Bali, in a splendid garden overlooking the sea, stands the holiday home built to incorporate the local design aesthetic. The house features large pavilions that open onto verandas, crowned with broad roofs and organized around courtyards with intricately decorated gates.

Right and opposite In the garden designed by landscape architect Michael White, lanterns and Balinese wood sculptures of deities are scattered everywhere.

Above and opposite The terraces, covered in parts and open in others, have stunning views of the garden and the sea beyond. The furnishings are Balinese, made by island craftsmen.

Right, above The veranda of the guest bungalow, where breakfast is served.

Right, below A gateway with decorative elements made out of straw underlines the close link between nature and architecture so characteristic the island's buildings.

Opposite The master bedroom, dominated by a wonderful antique bed, under a luxurious canopy held up by brightly coloured carved wooden pillars.

RALF OHLETZ

Interior design by Jaya Ibrahim

On the one hand, Singapore is an outpost of the West in the East, but on the other it is also an extraordinary repository of artistic and cultural history. Ralf Ohletz's apartment, in the heart of the business district near the War Memorial Park and St Andrew's Cathedral, helps to keep this heritage alive. It is a collector's house: the calm, modern spaces have been arranged with strict symmetry and filled with antique furnishings and rare design pieces, and form the ideal backdrop to the many works of art and crafts that the owner has collected over the years.

Right In the living room, facing the Raffles Hotel, an eleventh-century Javanese Buddha sits amid lamps and candlesticks that were designed by Jaya Ibrahim, who was also the creative force behind hotels for GHM Hotels and Aman Resorts, as well as private residences.

Above On the wall of the living room hangs a work by a Korean artist. The Chinese altar table dates from the Ming dynasty (1368–1644); atop sits a sculpture of a horse from the Han dynasty (206 BC–220 AD), along with two stone vessels, also from the Ming period.

Opposite One of the living room's most prominent design features is a seventeenth-century Japanese screen. On the table below are Chinese brush holders made from *huanghuali*, a wood from the rosewood family. The wicker armchair is by Jaya Ibrahim, while the Chinese table in the foreground is an antique from the Qing dynasty (1644–1911).

Left A triptych of panels hangs above a Qing day bed and form part of a Japanese screen, some sections of which decorate the living room. Four eagle feather fans with ivory handles, framed on Chinese silk, are arranged by the sides of the screen. The lamps are all by Jaya Ibrahim.

Below The bathroom, with its mosaic-tiled surfaces.

Overleaf The study, seen from the living room. The four-door cupboard is Chinese, from the Qing dynasty (1644–1911); other Chinese works of art are arranged on the very long, double desk. The rugs are nineteenth-century Chinese.

MIN MIN AUNG

Left A quirky sculpture of a hand, made from teak, adds a humorous touch to a door.

Right The house was originally built primarily in teak, reflecting the traditional building material of the area.

This nineteenth-century house in Nyaung-U, a town five kilometres from the holy city of Old Bagan – now Bagan Myothit – is the home of Min Min Aung, the owner of a traditional lacquer workshop. The entire structure was made of wood (mostly teak, some of which is wonderfully carved) because of the local custom that only temples can be constructed in stone.

Above, left and right The kitchen boasts traditional wooden bowls and utensils. Alongside the containers and vessels are two exquisitely carved wooden rosettes.

Opposite Every detail of the house, from the wall panelling to the furniture, has been made from richly carved teak.

Left Burmese lacquer objets d'art are scattered throughout the house, testament to the owner's trade.

Opposite The intricately worked teak balustrade is very fine, as are the sculptures, which at one time were reserved almost exclusively for members of religious orders and the aristocracy.

TUGU MALANG

Interior design by Anhar Setjadibrata

Left A carved anthropomorphic candlestick is shown to great effect against the brightly coloured wall, decorated with embossed flowers.

Right Exuberant, pink elephant-shaped terracotta fountains deliver water to the fish pond.

A fantastic Javanese house, complete with loggias, terraces and pagoda roofs and concealed in an enchanting Malang garden, has been restructured by that passionate lover of the oriental past, Anhar Setjadibrata. The designer has created a narrative of Indonesian history and mythology, room by room, through sculptures, handicrafts and works of art. The highlight of the house is the Apsara suite, dedicated to two kings: Jayawarnan II, an enlightened eighth-century sovereign; and Suryawarman II, who built Angkor Temple in Cambodia in the thirteenth century, where two thousand Apsara dancing nymphs, carved on the walls, pay homage to gods, kings and heroes.

Right In the Romeo and Juliet suite, a lamp featuring a Venetian mask provides dramatic illumination to cushions covered with Tibetan fabric.

Opposite Twelfth-century carved shutters, inlaid with coloured glass, feature prominently in the spa.

Above, left The bathroom in the Apsara suite, inspired by the bathing rituals of medieval Indonesian princes. The stone fountain represents Lembu Andini, Shiva's messenger.

Above, right At the entrance to the Tirta Gangga room, with its Hindu–Balinese atmosphere, stands a wooden statue of a guardian.

Opposite A magnificent four-poster bed, also in the Apsara suite, is framed by antique Indian pillars, mounted on seventeenth-century stone bases.

Above One of the intimate dining spaces in the restaurant.

Left This small dining room is lit by a multitude of lanterns. The restaurant continues in mirrors.

Left An antique sculpture fits snugly into a niche in a private room on the first floor.

Opposite The small sofas in the private rooms were inspired by the opium dens of the 1930s.

JOHN RIFENBERG

Designed by John Rifenberg

Left In a corner of the living room, fragments from a Burmese gilded wood sculpture form a frame for a mirror. The nineteenth-century silver vases were made in Thailand.

Right An eleventh-century Cambodian bronze mask sits atop a pedestal, next to a portrait of King Rama II, in a corridor leading to the dining room.

This Bangkok apartment belongs to John Rifenberg, a German architect who has lived for years in the Thai capital. The space is very large – 288 square metres – and is decorated using neutral colours and materials and diffused light, testament to the owner's love of Asian art and atmosphere.

Right, above The dressing room, leading to the bathroom with its teak-covered walls. The stone statue is Chinese.

Right, below A view through to the corridor, seen from the dining room.

Opposite Behind the Chinese stone statue, which dates from the early nineteenth century, is a mural painted in the Thai style by Chavalit Oumsiri.

Above A Chinese stone statue from the early nineteenth century.

Right The master bedroom with teak-panelled walls, seen from the dressing room. The antique furniture is Chinese.

Above and opposite The dining-room table is lit by a blown-glass chandelier and surrounded by chairs with Vienna straw backs, and is laid with valuable hand-painted Thai porcelain.

PASCALE NIVELLE

Designed by Antonio Ochoa Piccardo

The designer of this house – Antonio Ochoa Piccardo – is, although Venezuelan by birth, one of the best architects in Beijing (his cantilever house at Shuiguan is famous). Until recently home to Pascale Nivelle, *Libération*'s China correspondent, and her husband Charlie, the building harmoniously combines the traditional structure of the Peking courtyards (*siheyuan*) with a sense of contemporary lifestyle and a touch of Zen lyricism. Although it is new and designed with modern comforts in mind, the house seems to belong to the past, from the view over one of the small *hutongs* (lanes) of Beijing that have survived modernization to the old wooden roof covered with traditional curved tiles, and the centuries-old front doors to the ancient stones that divide up the interior spaces. Everything in the house, even though it has been reclaimed and spruced up, contributes the impression of a building immersed in a time that no longer exists.

Left The main door to the house was made from a reclaimed gate, taken from an old rural building.

Opposite A view of the corridor from which the various rooms radiate. The desk and chair were made in Beijing to the owners' design.

Above The roof is made from the curved tiles so characteristic of the area.

Left In the living room a dongas wooden screen modulates the light. The sloping roof with its wooden trusses is original, while the stove, integrated with radiant floor heating, is Danish and the furniture and accessories are from Ikea. The photograph on the wall is by Gilles Sabrie, a French photographer who lives in the Chinese capital. 'He is a dear friend,' says Nivelle, 'but we only found out on the Internet that he lived here.'

Opposite and right Two further views of the house show the decorative expressiveness of the contrast between stone and wood. The photographs are by Gilles Sabrié.

THE HOUSE ON THE MOUNTAIN

Designed by Victoria Sala

We are 180 kilometres from Beijing, in the middle of a succession of green hills and misty, even greener valleys. The Great Wall and the scattered roofs of the village of Huangtangkou are in sight. This house is the work of Victoria Sala, an English designer who moved to China years ago and has mixed old and new with balance and harmony, expressing the modern as a natural continuation of the traditional. Here, therefore, she has added three elongated buildings parallel to a structure, also elongated, which is over two hundred years old. The sloping roof is covered with the traditional tiles of Chinese and Japanese buildings, and the windows of the modern extension have been kept free of screens and lattices.

Right The four buildings that comprise the complex can be seen at the end of the lane. The oldest structure is identified by a drum that has been placed over the threshold, while the three newly built structures have architectural references that fit in well with the original building.

The entrance staircase, marked by
two antique urns, leads to the modern
buildings, which have been arranged
in accordance with the slope of the
mountainside.

The axis from the hallway to the staircase crosses the first of the new buildings, which discreetly exhibits the concrete and brick coatings employed for earthquake protection. The rugs, laid on the floor of rush matting, were made in the nineteenth century in Tibet and Kashgar.

Above This small living room has been given a touch of decorative distinction by a regional costume.

Right Dominant features of the living room include the large, modern fireplace and the landscape, framed by the full-height windows.

Overleaf Old and new combine in the living room, where an ancient Tibetan cabinet full of terracotta equestrian figures and a Buddhist altar table meet European-style furniture from Sala's company Livima Home.

Above, left and right Two views of the
garden, which, sheltered by an ancient
stone wall, separates the original
building from the new additions.

Opposite In front of the entrance to the
house, Sala has created an inviting,
minimalist terrace.

BAMBOO HOUSE

Designed by Kengo Kuma

Japanese architect Kengo Kuma has interpreted this large Chinese house (more than 700 square metres) in two ways. The first is the so-called 'Great Wall effect', a continuous wall of material that encircles the whole building and creates a homogeneous relationship with the setting, while the second is the choice of bamboo as the building material. 'A solution that does not challenge the landscape,' Kuma explains, 'but, on the contrary, takes up and reinterprets its "roughness", with the aim of generating a feeling of harmony.' Inside, bamboo remains dominant, covering the load-bearing structure of glass and cement. By playing with the spacing of the bamboo canes, Kuma is able to modulate light and transparency in total harmony with the Taoist simplicity of the furnishings.

Right The exterior of the Bamboo House is completely covered with a rhythmic series of bamboo canes, which have been mounted on sliding panels to match the windows.

The top of the staircase, leading down to the sleeping area: the local stone covering the floor creates a decorative contrast with the bamboo. On the left is the courtyard at the entrance to the house.

Above The anteroom's bamboo floor offers a welcome massage to tired feet.

Right In the dining room, large windows are screened by a dense mesh of bamboo canes, creating a play of light and shadow.

Overleaf Seen through the wall of glass in the living room, the surrounding vegetation seems to form part of the house's decorative scheme.

The entrance, with its two stone-clad steps to offset the slope of the land, is covered with an airy bamboo roof.

Above Bamboo is the central design feature, even in the bathroom.

Left In the bedroom, Kuma has interwoven two cultures by combining Japanese tatami mats with the refined simplicity of Chinese furniture.

TUGU LOMBOK

Interior design by Anhar Setjadibrata

Left A tribute to the Australian artist Donald Friend, who lived in Bali from 1968 to 1980.

Right Bale Kokok Pletok, seen from the beach. On the roof, the rooster and the snake represent Dewi Sri and her brother.

The Tugu Lombok complex is located on the gorgeous Indonesian island of Lombok, set within a six-hectare palm plantation that overlooks Sire Beach, a stretch of pure white sand on the northwest of the island with a view over the ocean and Mount Rinjiani. It is made up of various buildings – some of them ancient, others rebuilt with some original features – and incorporates references to Indonesian mythology, as seen at the Bale Kokok Pletok restaurant, which features ten caryatids representing Dewi Sri, the goddess of rice, who is worshipped by the people of Lombok. The expanse of water that stretches in front of the restaurant is the Infinity Pool, in which antique statues of the celestial guardians have been submerged.

Above The Infinity Pool and the beach,
seen from Bale Kokok Pletok.

Opposite Lamps set between the
caryatids are made of *kunai* grass.

Right, above and below The roofs of the huts are made from traditional *kunai* grass. Outside, cushions have been arranged for relaxation in the open air.

Opposite The Infinity Pool and the beach at sunset.

This outdoor bathroom in front of the Bhagavat Gita building boasts an ocean view. The bath, carved from an enormous river boulder, is tiled inside with a mosaic of coloured marble, while a bamboo screen provides some privacy.

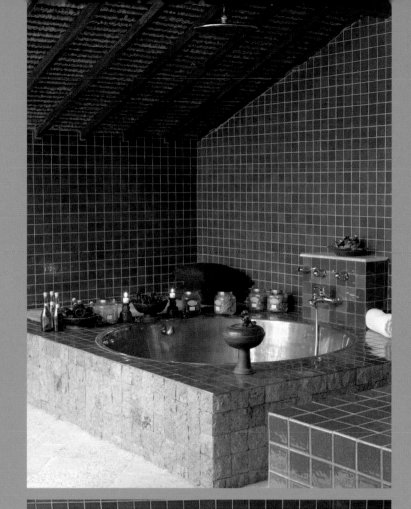

Right, above and below The enormous bathtub, in the outside bathroom of the Aloon-Aloon villa, is lined with copper.

Opposite An antique four-poster bed overlooks the garden. Veils of gauze protect sleepers from the unwanted advances of nighttime insects.

Above Small votive candles add a
decorative touch to a Balinese bench.

Right The beach and ocean, as seen
from one of the villas.

TENGKU ISMAIL

Left Typical features of a traditional Terengganu house include niches and distinctive moulding, as seen here. There are two types of Terengganu house, the *rumah kuala ibai* and the *rumah seberang baroh*, which differ in the type of gabled roof (the roof of the former is steeper than the latter), and in the division of the internal space (the *rumah kuala ibai* has six to eight columns, while the *rumah seberang baroh* has twelve to sixteen).

Right A view of the wooden houses with gabled roofs that make up Pura Tanjung Sabtu, the home of Tengku Ismail bin Tengku Su. At one time, Sultan Zainal Abidin III of Terengganu stayed here.

Pura Tanjung Sabtu is a collection of traditional Terengganu houses made of wood with steep, gabled roofs, located on the Nerus River, not far from Kuala Terengganu, an important seaside centre on the east coast of Malaysia. Together they comprise the home of Tengku Ismail bin Tengku Su, a well-known designer of jewelry and *songket*, the typical headdress of the area. Between 1992 and 1996, Tengku Ismail bought a row of abandoned houses and dismantled them, retaining their component parts. From other ruined buildings he acquired wooden walls, columns and ceramic tiles, and finally reassembled all of it, recreating a Terenggau village from centuries past.

Above and opposite The living room's intimate atmosphere is a decorative mix of various cultures, with its cultured eclecticism rooted in the style of the historic centre of Kuala Terengganu.

Overleaf Nature is an integral part of the architecture of Tengku Ismail's home. Large openings onto the loggia (*serambi*, in the local language) give the garden a leading role in the interior design. The large, open umbrellas inside enhance the outdoor feel of the space.

Above One of the terraces, which stretch out into the garden. The park, full of palms, bamboo, mango and Rengas trees, covers approximately seven hectares.

Opposite Along with the steep, gabled roof, the traditional Terengganu house is characterized by staggered levels that generate surprising spaces.

Above and left The master bedroom is dominated by a four-poster bed, covered by a mosquito net, which stands on a solid teak base.

BATH HOUSE RESIDENCE

Interior design by Zhang Jin Jie

Left Behind the screen, a massage therapy mattress invites relaxation. On the low table are lotions and oils for treatments, produced by the spa.

Right The indoor oval pool resembles a lake in a heavenly garden; above is an airy, tangled bunch of branches, almost a natural sculpture.

Overleaf View of the main hall of the spa, looking towards the stairs that lead to the Green T. House. On the right is the suspended treatment pavilion.

The Bath House Residence in Beijing was set up in 2009 as part of the Green T. House Living lifestyle project – Green T. House (see p. 216) opened in 1997 – at the instigation of Zhang Jin Jie, known as JinR, the eclectic and revolutionary 'empress' of Chinese taste. Inspired by the thermal pavilions of the Tang dynasty (626–907), Jin Jie reinvented the Zen bathing experience in a contemporary way, reflecting the sophisticated simplicity of metropolitan lofts and incorporating references to the natural world. 'My love for the Tangs comes from a love of simplicity, which is the heart of the Chinese tea culture,' explains Jin Jie. In 2009, Bath House Residence won the Spa of the Year category in the Asia Spa Awards.

Above Taking pride of place in the
main hall is Ron Arad's blue Victoria &
Albert sofa for Moroso. Hanging from
the ceiling are sets of projectors for
chromotherapy.

Opposite The simple serenity of the
treatment pavilion.

Above, left and right The stark forms of
the wash basins and staircase have a
monumental quality.

Opposite Behind the swathe of curtains
is the hydrotherapy room. Light is
diffused through the high windows and
is reflected onto the stone floor.

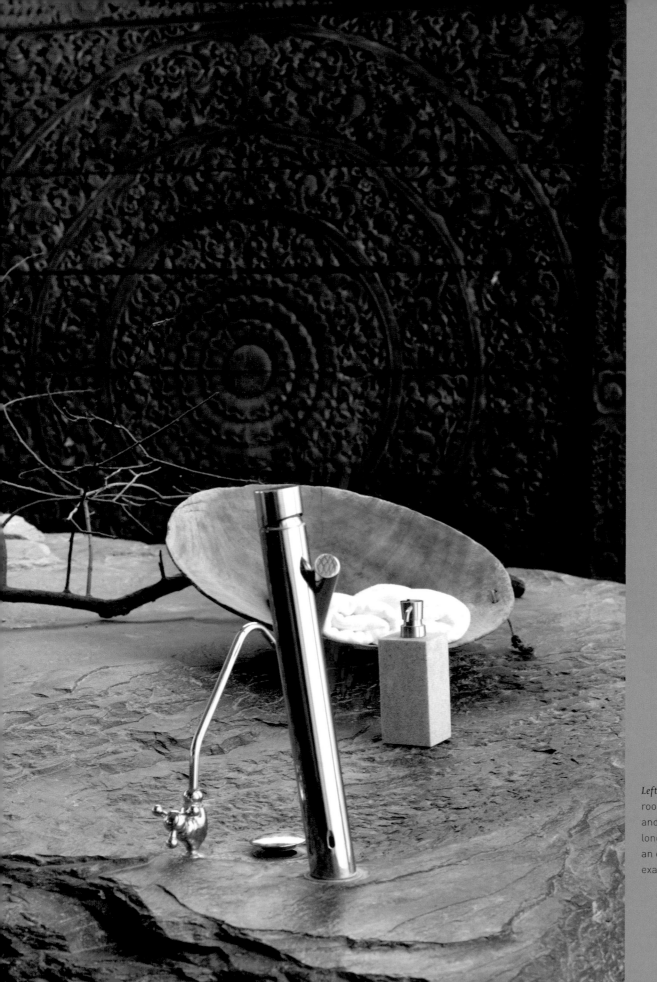

Left and opposite In the hydrotherapy room, a shell-shaped wooden bowl and designer accessories sit on the long, stone table. Against the wall is an ornately carved gate, an exquisite example of Chinese craftsmanship.

WANG LI

Anyone seeking an example of a traditional Chinese urban home should stop by this Beijing 'courtyard house', next to the Forbidden City. Although in form and plan the house appears as though it could have been built in the Qing dynasty (1644–1911), it is, in fact, brand new and designed for modern comfort. It stands on a raised platform above a swimming pool and cinema room, and is arranged around a colonnaded patio in classical symmetry. There are many evocative suggestions of architectural history, from the gabled roofs, covered in traditional tiles, and carved decorations on the portico, to the animal-shaped stones that guard the entrance and the large, stone panel that has been carved with special symbols to keep evil spirits at bay.

Above The stairs and passageway lead from street level to the living area.

Right The courtyard, looking towards the access lane, or *hutong*. The symbolic carved and gilded decorations embellishing the peristyle that surrounds the courtyard are worthy of note.

The south-facing living quarters harmoniously complement the entrance to the property. A feeling of balance is enhanced by the careful arrangement of the plants, and the red of the frames is another traditional touch.

Above and left The large and elegantly furnished living room reflects the owner's love of collecting. The low table in front of the sofa, made by Livima Home, a producer of European-style furnishings in China (see The House on the Mountain; p. 112), was fashioned from a recycled front door. Above the Jiangxi day bed hangs a richly carved wooden window shutter. In the room beyond, an antique wooden box is decorated with animal reliefs.

Above, left and right A second entrance to the property is also protected by a pair of carved stone 'guardians'.

Opposite A glimpse of the entrance from the *hutong*. In front of the door, two guardian lions ward off evil spirits. The extensive use of brickwork is in keeping with local building practice.

Left, above and below The second entrance, on the north side of the house, is oriented according to the principles of feng shui.

Opposite In front of the north entrance, access to the courtyard is partially blocked by a large, carved stone slab bearing phrases designed to confuse evil spirits – who can only move horizontally – and to encourage them to leave the house.

THE HOUSE OF A TEA MASTER

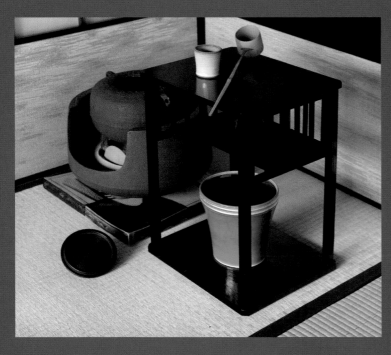

Left To the side of the stove (*furo*), on which the teapot (*kama*) has been put to boil, is the water basin (*mizusashi*), used to fill the *kama* or to wash the cup (*chawan*).

Right The corridor, which leads guests to the tea room, overlooks the garden.

According to Japanese tradition, the tea house, or *chashitsu*, is the building in which the tea ceremony, conducted under the guidance of the tea master, takes place, and is designed to achieve aesthetic and intellectual balance. At this tea master's house, the *chashitsu* is of the Daime type, with three tatami mats and supplemented by the room for the ceremony, the *zangetsutei*. A veranda overlooking the garden and a room for preparing food, the *mizuya*, completes the scene.

The tea ceremony room, made familiar to Westerners through the films of Yasujiro Ozu, Tomu Uchida and Kozaburo Yoshimura.

Above and left Cushions on the floor of the tea room await guests. The Chinese writer Lao She devoted his masterpiece *Cha Guan* (1958) to the ritual. In the novel, a group of people tell their life stories in the serene atmosphere of a tea house.

Above The entrance to the tea house.

Opposite The tea room is characterized by simple, clear shapes, which introduce a note of serenity. Everything in the house recalls nature, from the wood, to the rice paper of the movable panels (*shoji* if translucent, *fusuma* if opaque), to the natural fibre of the mats. They are expressions of a philosophy that urges a seamless and intimate connection with our surroundings.

YOT BON

There are many Buddhist monks who live in Siem Reap – with 83,000 inhabitants, one of Cambodia's largest cities. The reason for this religious concentration is Angkor, an area of over 400 square kilometres, which, from the ninth to the fifteenth centuries, was the centre of the Khmer empire; it is now an Unesco World Heritage Site. Inside this archaeological space, punctuated by many ruined temples, stands Angkor Wat, the only temple that has been in continuous use throughout the centuries. Among the monks who make the area their home is Yot Bon, whose house is sparsely furnished, as befitting a monk who has turned his back on worldly goods, but is full of delight and colour.

Right The exterior of the home of the monk, Yot Bon. Next to the wooden structure is a remnant of Angkor's former splendour.

In the prayer room, two colourful altars are covered with devotional gifts and prayers.

Right Yot Bon's bed is hidden behind a curtain of saffron yellow, the colour of the robes of a Buddhist monk.

Opposite The entrance to the house reflects the simplicity of the monk's life. The floor, also of wood, is laid upon the bare ground.

Overleaf The house also offers shelter to the marginalized people of Siem Reap. A simple pump provides water for washing and cooking.

HIROYUKI SHINDO

The village of Kita, sixty kilometres north of Kyoto, came under the aegis of the Japanese historical monuments association in 1993 due to the many ancient buildings within its confines. This house, belonging to Hiroyuki Shindo, is perhaps the largest and most valuable among them. It dates back to the Edo period (1603–1853), specifically 1796, when it was built by a carpenter from the Wkasa district.

Above The roof is reinforced with a series of 'saddles', made of chestnut, through which the ridgepole has been threaded. There are seven of these saddles; the number is not accidental, and refers to the high social rank of the first owner.

Right Wooden walkways are a typical feature of traditional Japanese houses.

Above Sliding doors reveal the verdant garden that surrounds the house. The wooden walkway, or *engawa*, encircles the living space.

Opposite The furniture in this guest room is the work of local craftsmen.

Overleaf A view of the guest room with the bed positioned in the centre of the room. In accordance with local tradition, the type of staircase seen here (a *haku-kaidan*) is used as both a wardrobe and as a means of connecting to the bathroom above.

197

Above One of the main rooms of the house serves as an intimate gallery. The owner is a world-renowned artist, whose work has been exhibited at the Art Institute of Chicago, the Cleveland Museum of Art and the Israel Museum in Jerusalem, among others.

Right Shindo calls the gallery space 'Little Indigo Museum', a reference to his own work, which features prominently.

CARLO PESSINA

Interior design by Carlo Pessina

Artist and designer Carlo Pessina, who counts Ferrero, Lancia and Eaton among his many clients, both lives and works on Bali, where he has set up a flourishing furniture company. His house is at Sanur, on Bali's south-eastern coast, four hundred metres from the sea, in one of the island's most beautiful residential areas. The house is built in the traditional Balinese style, using local materials – palimanan sandstone, coco wood, *kunai* grass – and such typical features as natural pigment plaster and mosaic with pinnidae shell inlays. The house is made up of three elements: the main building; the guest pavilion; and the swimming pool and fitness area.

Left The gateway and walls of the entrance to the guest pavilion are made from paras, a Balinese stone; the statues of Balinese 'guardians' are made from sandstone.

Right To the right of the entrance to the master suite stands an imposing Kalimantan wood statue, while on the left, a Balinese carving hangs above a bench from Java. In the corner is an old Balinese gong, made from a single piece of wood, used by villagers as an alarm during emergencies.

Above The living room, seen from the master bedroom, contains an array of important and beautiful objects: on the left, in the foreground, is part of a boat from Madura Island; to the right is a day bed that started life as a Javanese loom, a table designed by Carlo Pessina, with pinnidae shell inlays, and an antique Javanese cabinet. Hanging on the wall is part of an antique staircase from Leti Island. The roof is made of *kunai* grass.

Opposite, above The lush garden is planted with palms, frangipani, bromeliads and orchids.

Opposite, below A view of the entrance.

Left Another view of the living room, with the floor criss-crossed by wooden inlays. Underneath the mirror, the console table, made from oxidized brass, is by Carlo Pessina, as are the coco wood chairs and oval dining table. The small wooden deer belonged to the collection of Donald Friend, an Australian painter who lived in Bali during the 1970s.

Opposite To the right of the doorway to the kitchen is a wooden animist symbol from Flores; next to it is an antique Javanese door, carved with figures from the *Ramayana* epic. On the other side of the doorway are two wooden figures in traditional Javanese costume.

Above The doorway leading to the inner living room is made of carved teak, and still bears traces of polychrome and gold leaf. The wood sculpture is from Borneo, and the panel on the far wall is from a house in Nias, in western Indonesia. The coco wood credenza is another of Pessina's designs.

Right In the Blue Guest Room (there is also a Yellow Guest Room) stands an antique Chinese bed of carved teak, along with a Balinese cabinet made of carved wood and decorated with gold leaf. The walls are decorated with blue and silver stencils of Balinese motifs; the antique door is Javanese.

An antique Javanese day bed with
elaborate carving is covered with a
Sumba blanket; on either side are
two Javanese cabinets that have been
painted in green and red and decorated
with gold leaf. Atop the left-hand cabinet
is an ancient Balinese statue from
Garuda.

Above A pathway of palimanan stone leads to an old Javanese house that has been left in its original condition. On the right is a fragment of a Chinese temple.

Right The open-air living room in the Blue Guest Room. The small palm and shell table and solid wood benches are Pessina's work, while the colonial lamp is Dutch.

Overleaf To the left of the swimming pavilion, a staircase leads up to the *bale*, Balinese for a frigidarium, or cold pool. Seen in the background to the right is the guest pavilion.

GREEN T. HOUSE

Interior design by Zhang Jin Jie

Left Vases and flowers have been arranged under designer Zhang Jin Jie's expert eye.

Right The main room of Green T. House, in which a woman serving tea is seen in silhouette.

Opening in 1997, Green T. House has become one of the most stylish restaurants and retreats in Beijing (see also Bath House Residence; p. 156). The pavilion takes its stylistic cue from the tea houses that were popular during the Qing dynasty (1644–1911). The tea culture in China is connected to philosophy and is subject to precise rituals, but Zhang Jin Jie, the owner and founder of Green T. House – and first female chef in the country – decided to break with thousand-year-old tradition and transformed the building into an homage to minimalism, eliminating everything superfluous and keeping only 'the poetic spirit of the mysterious ancient house': lots of white, geometric screens, a few pieces of simple, almost monastic furniture, silk lanterns and stoneware dishes and teapots, all designed by Jin Jie, who, on top of everything else, is also a musician, composer and artist.

Above A low table and straw cushions echo the simplicity that is a theme throughout the restaurant.

Left Ultra-modern meets traditional: the mirrored glass and reflective surfaces of the modern shapes are a striking contrast to the antique cabinet.

Another view of the main room, which is protected by screens of pure white that filter the light. The polished concrete floor sparkles under hand-painted silk lanterns.

Above An evocative wood sculpture dominates the long corridor that runs alongside the main room. On one side are stark white screens; on the other, austere black panels.

Opposite At the head of the long table is a chair – more of an artwork – titled *There Is No Chair*, and designed by Jin Jie.

Left, above A corner in the main room is reserved for tea and quiet reflection.

Left, below Continuing the predominant colour scheme of the building, the four-poster bed is flanked by white screens and covered in pale cushions and gauze.

Opposite An enormous birdcage contains a branch of purest white.

THE HOUSE OF A MONK

One rainy day
far away from the capital
my house with the peach trees
now in flower.

Yosa Buson (1716–83)

This simple wooden house has the appearance of one that is distant, separate from the jumbled modernity of the metropolis. An unchanging island, a moment of respite in the breathlessness of life: its historic role as a fulcrum of the community lies in the past, but its existence as the living memory of a great spiritual tradition does not. Measurements, proportions and colours invite meditation; the garden, water features and stones lift one's thoughts to the eternal; the simplicity and emptiness are not a decorative wasteland but represent continuity and timelessness. This, after all, is the house of a Shinto monk.

Right A garden tended with care and skill leads up to the Meiji-inspired house, characterized by a carved wooden porch. Two large basins collect rainwater for irrigation, against a background of commemorative and funerary stones dedicated to the ancestors, considered deities in the Shinto religion.

Above The domestic space, or *ima*, can
be partitioned as needed with movable
panels of wood and opaque rice paper
(*fusuma*).

Opposite The heart of the house, a
multi-purpose space furnished with the
simplicity and purity befitting a monk.
In the centre, surrounded by cushions
(*zabuton*), is a brazier, carved from
abtree trunk.

Overleaf Embellished with devotional
gifts, the altar is used for the daily
prayers required by the Shinto faith, the
dominant religion in Japan.

Preceding pages Another view of the *ima*. On the left, a section of a tree trunk, carefully polished, is a representation of one of the Shinto gods.

Left The roof, which considerably overhangs the edge of the house, is made from tiles known as *kawara*.

Above The guest room, with the typical low table (*zataki*) and cushions. A decorative panel (*kakejiku*) hangs on the far wall, another typical element of a room that interprets traditional features with a certain decorative modernity.

JÉRÔME ABEL SEGUIN

Designed by Jérôme Abel Seguin

For his own Balinese villa, the French sculptor and designer Jérôme Abel Seguin decided to bend the local rules and opt for a 'nineteenth-century-industrial-workshop style', in which only the pulleys, hoists and tools are antiques and everything has been created from scratch. The house stands in a non-tourist area of Bali, in what used to be a rice field, and is reflected in a swimming pool surrounded by palms.

Right The villa by night, as seen from the side of the swimming pool, which is clad in grey stone with Java and paras stone from Bali. The garden has been planted with palms and pandanus trees. Visible in the centre of the house, the dining room looks like a wide corridor.

Above In the living room, the chairs and coffee table were designed by Seguin and made from Borneo wood.

Opposite, above The narrow strip between the house and the perimeter wall has been filled with agaves and cacti.

Opposite, below The central dining area features furniture designed by Seguin, using reclaimed materials. Against the walls, silver-plated pulleys rest on nineteenth-century Chinese pedestal tables. In the background, the outer wall can be seen, lined with palm trees.

Opposite and below The entrance is via a gallery lined with a colonnade of thirty reclaimed telegraph poles. Next to the low table, again designed by Seguin, are two Javanese chairs.

Left Another view of the entrance and the living room.

Above The stools and table were all designed by Seguin.

JIMBARAN BAY

Interior design by Anhar Setjadibrata

This resort complex on Bali overlooks Jimbaran Bay, which is famous for its white sandy beaches. It is made up of many villas, built in typical Balinese style with roofs thatched in *kunai* grass, scattered along terraces that at one time contained rice fields. Each villa is submerged in the vegetation and has an internal courtyard; many have private pools, whereas a shared infinity pool seems to stretch out into the ocean.

Right The entrance to one of the villas, framed by its tropical garden.

Above A bedroom in one of the villas, furnished with locally made furniture.

Opposite Seen from inside, a gabled roof of *kunai* grass is typical of the building traditions of the area.

A bathroom built for two: the basins have been carved out of local stone, and water spurts out of bamboo shower heads above.

Left One of the villas by night, its two storeys romantically reflected in the infinity pool.

Overleaf Water lilies and lotus flowers grow in the small, overhanging pond.

TUGU BALI
Designed by Anhar Setjadibrata

This complex of buildings raised on pilings and facing the ocean is a compendium of Indonesian history. It was designed by Anhar Setjadibrata, and is made up of twenty-six villas whose design pays homage to the successive civilizations that have thrived here. Among the villas is the Bale Sutra, or Palace of Harmony, a painstaking reconstruction of an eighteenth-century Chinese temple; a suite inspired by the life of the Belgian poet Adrien-Jean Le Mayeur de Meprès, who lived here between 1932 and 1958; and a pavilion named for Walter Spies, a German painter and musician who settled in Indonesia in 1928.

Right In the garden is a statue of Boma, a guardian of local legend who protects Balinese houses from evil spirits.

Opposite A corner of the Palace of Harmony, which was transported here piece by piece. Today it is used as a restaurant featuring *peranakan* cuisine, a fusion of Chinese and Indonesian cooking.

Overleaf The swimming pool and garden.

Above The Palace of Harmony, where meals are eaten underneath the gaze of Balinese heroes. This room symbolizes the harmony between Chinese and Balinese cultures.

Right, above A guardian figurine protects the dining table.

Right, below On a table in the Wardeng hut sits a jar and a pair of oil lamps.

Above In this large bathroom, guests can bathe in water perfumed with flower petals. Straw tatami mats and cushions are arranged across the floor.

Opposite A bath and massage bed in the Rejang suite, with its veranda overlooking the ocean.

Above A guardian deity seen in striking silhouette against the ocean waves.

Left The Waroeng hut, where guests can enjoy meals according to Indonesian rituals, is decorated with local furnishings.

VILLA DE LA PAIX
Designed by Bill Bensley

The Villa de la Paix at Siem Reap, Cambodia recalls the ancient Khmer civilization that flourished between the ninth and fifteenth centuries a few miles away in the temple-city of Angkor. Pure white, sumptuous, and profoundly linked to tradition, this house, designed by Bill Bensley of Bensley Design Studios, pays homage to the ancient city, starting with the façade, so reminiscent of a temple with its illuminated torchères and enigmatic sculpture of a sacred Apsara dancer in front of the main entrance. Both inside and out, Art Deco references are interspersed with elements inspired by Khmer art and the austerity of Japanese design.

Right In the inner courtyard, an ancient fig tree grows in the centre of a torch-lit pond.

Above, left and opposite The living room is sandwiched between a double colonnade and is furnished with a series of rocking couches.

Left An external colonnade.

Opposite The dining room has low tables and mats in the Japanese style, while the wall's niches and bands of black and white were inspired by the architecture of the Khmer empire.

Right In the entrance corridor is a statue of an Apsara dancer, a traditional form of dance that is sacred to the gods.

Top and above This bed boasts a striking, decorative bed head; the bathroom can be glimpsed just beyond.

Left A corner of the spa, with treatment beds and specially designed lanterns.

Overleaf Next to the swimming pool is a corner for relaxation. On the wall are reliefs that represent the tree of life, inspired by Khmer art.

JOANNA CROSS

Left In a corner of the living room, a statue of a Burmese priest sits atop an antique sedan chair.

Right A wide veranda runs along the front of the house. The cart, which at one time would have been pulled by buffalo, comes from the north of Thailand.

More than a residence, this series of buildings forms the 'cluster house' so typical of Thai architecture – a living arrangement that is especially common in the countryside and is designed to house different generations of a single family together. Some of the buildings are modern, others are ancient structures. All are made of teak, as tradition requires, and come from the countryside north of Bangkok. They were dismantled, transported on barges and reassembled here to a design by Jim Thompson, who planned the wide, raised veranda, around which are centred two smaller houses and a large living room. The owner Joanna Cross lives in one of these smaller buildings, surrounded by furniture and works of art collected by her mother, the antiquarian collector Connie Mangskau.

Right, above Next to the door that opens onto the veranda stands a richly carved and decorated Thai teak cabinet.

Right, below A detail of the living room, with statue of a gilded, seated Buddha.

Opposite Two imposing eighteenth-century statues of Buddha and a nineteenth-century sculpture of a kneeling Burmese monk dominate the large living room.

Overleaf A twelfth-century Khmer sculpture and a Laotian drum are arranged in front of the central pillar of the living room, while a nineteenth-century Thai painting hangs on the wall behind a table of carved teak.

Above Two sculpted doors from an ancient temple have been placed either side of a small, gilded shrine. On the wall are carved teak panels.

Left A four-poster bed in elaborately carved and painted teak.

Above On the balcony, a ninth-century Buddha rests on a small Thai altar.

Opposite One of the several 'spirit houses' in the garden. Flowers, incense and votive offerings are placed in front of them each day.

M. L. TRI DEVAKUL

Designed by M. L. Tri Devakul

Left A pathway, leading to a Buddhist temple.

Right Two pavilions at the top of a hill, one closed and one open. A cascade of water falls from a small lake on top the hill, along a channel down three descending basins.

The house and garden of M. L. Tri Devakul, a well-known Thai architect, educated at Harvard, is at Kata Beach, one of the most beautiful corners of the island of Phuket. The original bungalow remains and has been transformed into a pavilion, with a views overlooking the sea. Over time, Devakul designed additional airy structures with *kunai* grass roofs, a saltwater swimming pool and a small temple dedicated to Buddha. The garden, also created by the architect, seems to be a well-organized, miniature jungle.

The long, rectangular dining table in the pavilion has been covered with local tiles. Above it, antique Thai cooking pots and pans hang from the *kunai* grass ceiling. On the right, the doors have been fashioned from bamboo cane.

Right At the top of the hill, a tranquil fish pond sits between the two pavilions. In the foreground is a sculpture of a buffalo from northern Thailand, lit by outdoor lamps that have been mounted on the trunks of sugar palm trees.

Overleaf The terrace, with its large, saltwater swimming pool.

MICHITAKA HIROSE

Designed by Kengo Kuma

Left The house is clad in a skin of corrugated steel, reminiscent of American transcontinental freight trains.

Opposite The detached staircase, covered with opalescent plastic, creates a sculptural effect.

This house in the hilly university area of Tokyo is a real architectural feat, as it cleverly provides logical yet poetic solutions to both the unfortunate topography – a plot of only two hundred square metres on a steep slope – and the demands of the owner, a renowned professor of computer science with a passion for model trains, as well as introducing order and beauty into the mishmash of the surrounding architecture. With American freight trains in mind, architect Kengo Kuma designed a stereometrically constructed shell, covered in sheets of corrugated steel that come to life in the sunlight, vibrating with light and shade. Inside, the staggered levels are connected by cantilevered staircases that create a feeling of movement, and the walls are covered with opalescent plastic that modulates and diffuses the light. Furnishings have been reduced to essentials, with the toy trains confined to an enormous storage cupboard lining an entire wall of the living room. All of this modernity is complemented by the traditional, in the form of a monastic room for the tea ceremony.

Above The austere room for the *chado*, or tea ceremony, is a step up from the wood floor of the entrance.

Opposite Two views of the staircase, which connects the different levels that allow the building to adapt to the sloping terrain. It is made from moulded metal, with an old fishing net serving as a handrail.

Overleaf The elongated living room-cum-studio takes its shape from railway carriages. The storage cupboard on the right houses the owner's model train collection, which ranges from old-fashioned locomotives to the bullet trains of the Shinkansen network. The austerity of the pure white lacquered furniture contrasts with the natural wood floor.

GOLDEN TRIANGLE RESORT
Designed by Bill Bensley

In a remote part of Thailand, between the Ruak and Mekong rivers, is the Golden Triangle resort, named after the Golden Triangle area on the borders of Myanmar, Laos and Thailand. Designed by architect Bill Bensley to provide maximum comfort while at the same time respecting nature and local traditions, the tented camp contains fifteen bungalows, each measuring ninety square metres, all with views over the rivers and outfitted with teak furniture and handmade fabrics, as well as a library, a spa, the Nong Yao restaurant, the Burma Bar and a cellar for wines from Thailand and across the globe.

Above Six elephants are available to take guests on jungle excursions.

Right One of the fifteen bungalows, overlooking the spectacular countryside.

Right Bathrooms, too, have ceilings of *kunai* grass, together with bamboo walls.

Opposite The fireplace in the Nong Yao restaurant is complemented by the traditional ceiling.

Overleaf This bungalow boasts both teak furniture and an impressive copper bathtub.

Left, above and below Everything you need for a perfumed bath, including scented flowers that have been scattered in the bath water.

Opposite The wooden bathtub is ready for relaxation on the veranda, screened by a gauzy mosquito net.

Overleaf A bungalow by night.

LARA DJONGGRANG RESTAURANT

Designed by Anhar Setjadibrata

The Lara Djonggrang Restaurant, designed and built by Anhar Setjadibrata, is right in the centre of Jakarta. It has three sections: the restaurant, La Bihzad Bar and the China Blue Restaurant. The Lara Djonggrang room was inspired by the Javanese legend of the eponymous princess, who lived in the ninth century and was tormented by the wicked Prince Bandung Bondowoso, who first murdered her father and then forced her to marry him. After initially escaping, Lara was turned into a stone statue by the prince, but was later saved following the intervention of the gods Sang Maha Dewa and Vishnu. La Bihzad Bar pays homage to the great sixteenth-century painter Kamal al-din Bihzad, whereas the China Blue Restaurant is decorated with antique Chinese furniture and objets d'art.

Above, left Two potiches from Afghanistan, used as water containers, sit underneath a Qing dynasty table from the mid-nineteenth century. The Chinese candlesticks were originally used during ceremonies to pray to ancestors.

Right The entrance to the Lara Djonggrang Restaurant and La Bihzad Bar, decorated with antique Javanese stone statues. The sculpture on the right is of Princess Lara, ascending to the heavens on the back of a mythological animal.

Above Inside the China Blue Restaurant, two Qing dynasty reliefs, each weighing about a ton, represent the guardian of the heavens. At the end of the table is an antique Buddha from Burma.

Opposite Next to the wall relief is a sculpture of a winged horse from Afghan mythology.

The corridor, partly outdoors, which leads to the Lara Djonggrang room and La Bihzad Bar. The red statues represent Lara's maids, who were instructed by the princess to cause enough of a commotion to waken the roosters and thus prevent Bandung Bondowoso from completing the task that would enable him to marry her. The oil lamps create an otherwise romantic atmosphere.

Opposite A statue of Lara Djonggrang, portrayed rejecting the advances of Bandung Bondowoso, her father's murderer. The door panels date from the Ming dynasty (1368–1644); the colonial lamps come from across the whole of Indonesia.

Above The corridor connecting La Bihzad Bar to the garden, covered with tiles found in old Dutch colonial houses. The stone benches and cushions mark a waiting area where cocktails are served, useful when the restaurant is full.

Above The teak ceiling of La Bihzad Bar is from an old Chinese temple. Below are two mythological lions, or *kilin*, along with a rice container from Sumatra made from a single piece of wood.

Right The Lara Djonggrang room decorated with Indonesian antiques, stone statues of Buddha from the centre of Java, terracotta reliefs from centuries-old temples, and a portrait of

Antique paintings of the god of thunder adorn the walls of the China Blue Restaurant, while a bronze Qing dynasty vase, a Ming dynasty porcelain plate and two cast-iron pillars of Dutch colonial origin, painted scarlet, add colour.

LOSARI COFFEE PLANTATION

Designed by Andrea and Fabrizio Magnaghi

The Losari complex is located in the centre of Java, in a working coffee plantation at an altitude of nine hundred metres. The villa, made up of various industrial buildings, dates from 1928, when a Dutch family decided to move here to grow coffee. The house was restored by Italian businesswoman Gabriella Teggia, who now lives in Indonesia, and has become a club house, surrounded by abandoned Javanese houses that have been transported here from across the island and redecorated in the Kudus style. The complex, like a real town, has four bars and restaurants, a train depot that has been converted into a room for parties, and a coffee warehouse, a swimming pool, fish pond and Turkish bath.

Above Some of the organic produce that is grown on the plantation.

Right An antique Javanese bed in the Losari Club House.

The relaxation area in the spa.

Above, left The Turkish bath.

Above, right and opposite Guest rooms
with four-poster beds in the Jogo Kudus
Villa, decorated in the Kudus style.

Above, left and right The fitness centre
is designed along the model of ancient
Turkish baths, with three pavilions, a
calidarium, a relaxation room and a
swimming pool.

Opposite The bamboo forest, the edges
of which are planted with highly fragrant
tuberoses.

M. L. POOMCHAI CHUMBALA

Interior and landscape design by M. L. Poomchai Chumbala

Interior designer M. L. Poomchai Chumbala has reinterpreted tradition in a modern way at his house in Bangkok, embellishing five interconnected pavilions with such details as reclaimed-wood cladding, gabled roofs decorated with ornamental finials, a raised entrance containing a small sunken garden, and warm interiors enlivened by richly carved panels and an exuberance of coloured and gilded objets d'art.

Above Books, glassware and small bronze sculptures have pride of place on a low lacquered table.

Opposite The dining room is used by the family on formal occasions, whereas everyday meals are eaten on the terrace or the lawn. The backlit display cabinet, with its splendid moulding from a Chinese screen, contains lacquer pieces commissioned by Queen Chiang Mai for a birthday.

Above An antique carved cabinet contains blue-and-white porcelain from China.

Right The living room is lit by windows that are surmounted by fanlights acquired from an Islamic-style house that had been demolished. Cushions covered in precious silk rest on the Chinese Chippendale armchairs.

Above, left The front steps, leading to
the entrance.

Above, right Platforms and terraces
appear to float above small ponds laid
out by the owner-designer.

Opposite Papyrus vases and bonsai
adorn a corner of the entrance
terrace.

Above Two stone sculptures of Buddha keep watch in the garden.

Left A small sunken garden, lush with ferns and bamboo, is set in the floor of the atrium.

Overleaf Even under the stairs, antique cabinets display precious collectibles.

A HOUSE IN ASAGAYA-MINAMI

Designed by Koji Ogawa

Koji Ogawa is a master of controlling the smallest dimensions. In the megacities of Japan, where two-thirds of the population live in cities that occupy barely one-twentieth of the country's land area (and in Tokyo in particular, where Ogawa does most of his work), this is a regular condition. Building plots are sometimes no larger than fifty square metres, and extremely strict anti-earthquake and aesthetic building regulations govern design. The solution is to go upwards, but not too far because of the height restrictions in residential areas. In this house, Ogawa, who counts Mies van der Rohe, Louis Kahn and Kenzo Tange among his influences, has taken on all of these challenges and come up with a small masterpiece that satisfies the contemporary requirements for comfort, as well as embracing the passions of the owner (art and music). The house is vertical, airy and full of light, rough but also harmonious, with board-marked concrete that resembles wood planks, simple wood floors, and satin glass that seems to be a logical extension of the wall colour.

Above A painting by Matsumoto Yoko.

Opposite A detail of the façade, with its reinforced concrete that echoes the wooden formwork of tatami mats. This austere yet elegant decoration is echoed by the interiors.

The large concrete partition wall in the living room has a structural function, but also introduces a strong design element that complements the abstract works of art both on the wall and propped up on the floor. The simplicity of the oak flooring is offset by the sofa by Robert Venturi for Knoll and a sculpture by Toya Shigeo. A glimpse of the garden breaks up the rigid asceticism of the décor.

343

Above One wall in the living room has been whitewashed, whereas the wall opposite has been covered in New Guinea walnut. The sofa is a modern design from Muji, and the chair is a Chinese antique.

Right In the living room, paintings by Georges Rouault contrast with the oak floorboards and Chinese and Korean antiques. In the foreground are two examples of Italian style: a reworked version of the Tolomeo lamp by Michele de Lucchi and Giancarlo Fassina for Artemide, and the Lola lamp by Alberto Meda and Paolo Rizzatto for Luceplan.

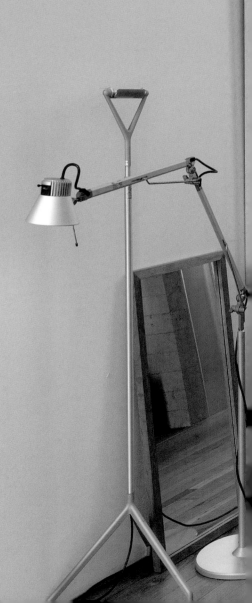

Left The owners wanted the master bathroom to be the space with the most light in the house, so it has been positioned on the second floor, where it receives light from the entrance below. The bath is covered in wood; the basin is set in a New Guinea walnut surround.

Opposite The entrance was designed to be a transition area between the external, public space and the intimate, private area of the domestic sanctuary: a kind of purification pool to wash away the clamour of the city. With its simple, steel handrail, the detached staircase has an abstract, sculptural look.

A feeling of elegance and calm is generated by the tatami mat flooring. The sliding wall of New Guinea walnut both separates the toilet and the bathroom from the rest of the space, and creates a strong, decorative effect.

VILLA TUGU

Interior design by Anhar Setjadibrata

At Canggu, a fishing town on the island of Bali, Villa Tugu takes visitors on a journey through the history, traditions and mythology of Indonesia and South East Asia via architectural and decorative choices. Objets d'art, handicrafts and sculpture give life to a kind of folklore pantomime in a style now known as 'Asian Bohemian'.

Right The entrance 'bridge' to the villa, suspended over a pond full of lotus flowers. Javanese leather puppets, or *wayang*, are hung on the pillars and are lit from behind at night, producing characteristic Indonesian shadow plays. The bronze Chinese candlesticks are a hundred years old.

Above Votive stone sculptures in the garden.

Opposite The lotus flower pond.

Above The table tops are made from Carrara marble.

Opposite The lamp bases on the console tables are nineteenth-century votive holders. Above hang paintings by the Chinese–Balinese artist Lim Kwi Bing, who used to live at Malang.

Above, left Two mythological Balinese horses, two centuries old, keep watch over the swimming pool, accompanied by three antique sculptures of praying monks from Burma.

Above, right A ceremonial gilded mask, used by Sumatran dancers, hangs on a green wall at the entrance.

Opposite In a guest room hangs a panel taken from an antique Gebyok screen, found in a Javanese house.

Overleaf At the bottom of the garden stands an enormous statue from Cambodia of the four-armed god Vishnu, protected by a large Burmese parasol.

First published in the United Kingdom in 2010 by
Thames & Hudson Ltd, 181A High Holborn,
London WC1V 7QX

www.thamesandhudson.com

First published in 2010 in hardcover in the United States of America by
Thames & Hudson Inc., 500 Fifth Avenue, New York, New York 10110

thamesandhudsonusa.com

Original edition © 2010 Magnus Edizioni Srl, Udine
Illustrations © 2010 Massimo Listri
This edition © 2010 Thames & Hudson Ltd, London

British Library Cataloguing-in-Publication Data
A catalogue record for this book is available from the British Library

Library of Congress Catalog Card Number 2010923383

ISBN: 978-0-500-51546-4

Printed and bound in Hong Kong